Contents

Before you start

About this book

All the masks in this book are simple to make from easy-to-find materials. Use the masks to pretend to be a wild animal, a funny clown or a grand king and many other exicitng ideas. Once you have learnt the basic rules of mask-making, you can enjoy creating more masks from your own designs.

Tools and materials

You will need paper plates, paints and a paintbrush for many of the projects. Gouache paints are the best because they are thick, dry fast and cover well.

You will also need scissors, glue and thin elastic for holding the masks on.

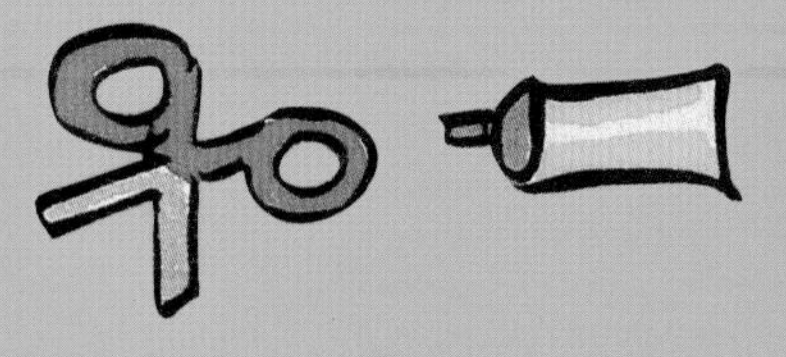

All the materials you will need are listed at the start of each project.

Make It Yourself

Masks

This edition published in 2006 by
Franklin Watts
338 Euston Road
London NW1 3BH

Franklin Watts Australia
Hachette Children's Books
Level 17/207 Kent Street
Sydney NSW 2000

Originally published by
Casterman, Belgium

Text and illustrations: Bernadette Theulet-Luzié
Photography: Gerard Vincon
Design: Dominique Mazy
Translation: Ruth Thomson

ISBN-10: 0 7496 6912 8
ISBN-13: 978 0 7496 6912 6

A CIP catalogue record for this book is
available from the British Library.

Dewey Classification: 731.75

Printed in China

Tips for making masks

How to make eye holes in the mask

1 Hold the mask up to your face. Ask an adult to mark the position of your eyes.

2 Cut out two eye holes. These should be about 6 cm apart.

How to wear the mask

Use either flat or round, thin elastic. Measure it around the back of your head.

flat elastic

round elastic

If you use flat elastic, staple the ends to the inside of the mask, just below the eye holes.

If you use round elastic, poke a hole on either side of the mask, just below the eye holes. Thread through the elastic and knot both ends.

Learning logos

The activities in the book provide practice in different skills, identified by the logos below.

An activity practising imagination and creativity

An activity practising fine motor control

An activity practising spatial skills

Monkey face

empty shoe box • ruler • pencil • three paper plates
scissors • glue • gouache paints • paintbrush

1 Measure and mark 25 cm on three sides of a box and cut off the rest of the box.

Put the box over your head and ask an adult to mark the position of your eyes. Take the box off and cut out two eye holes.

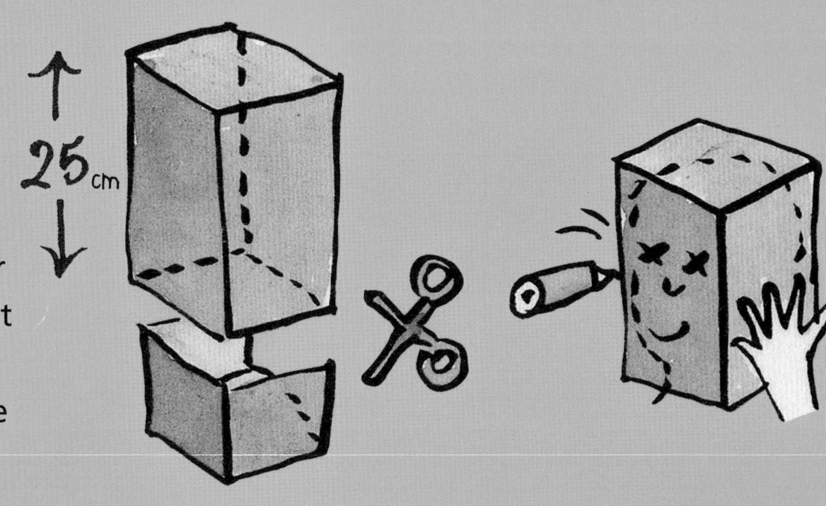

2 Glue a paper plate on to the box, just below the eye holes.

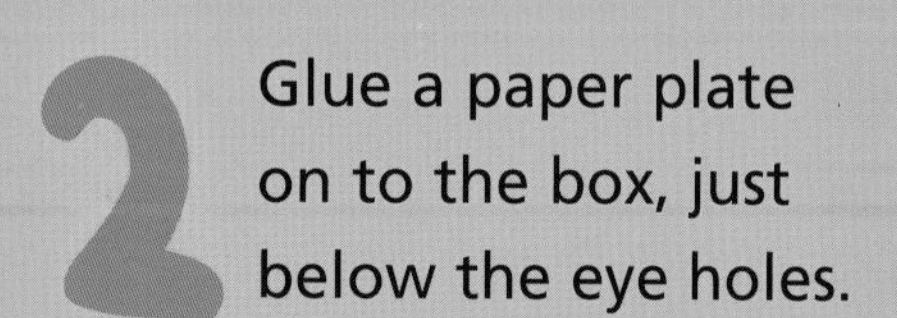

3 Cut the rims off two other plates, leaving two small circles.

Fold one side of both circles. Glue the folds to either side of the box to make ears.

4

Paint a monkey face with bushy eyebrows, large, wide nostrils and a smiling mouth.

Feathery bird

empty egg carton ● pencil ● scissors ● paintbrush
gouache paints ● coloured card ● glue ● elastic

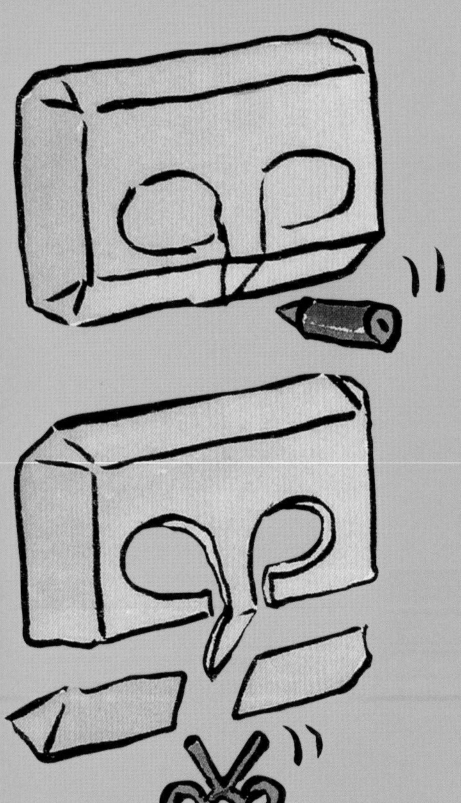

1 Cut off the top of an egg carton. Draw eye holes and a beak shape on it.

Cut them out.

2 Fold the beak to make space for your nose. Paint the beak yellow and the rest of the mask purple.

3 Cut out six feathers from brightly coloured card. Glue them on to either side of the mask, just above the eye holes.

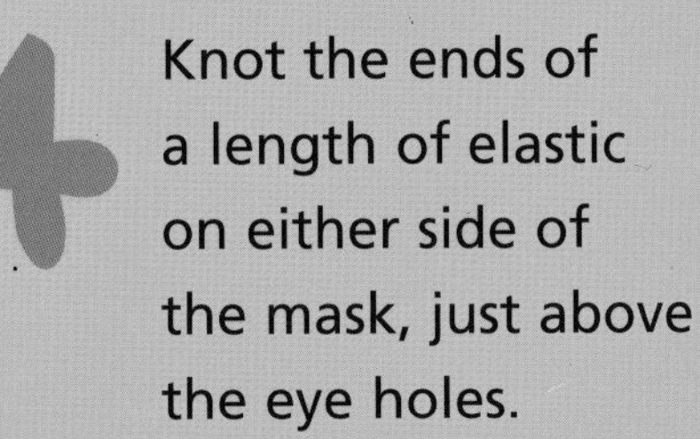

4 Knot the ends of a length of elastic on either side of the mask, just above the eye holes.

Friendly Frog

paper plate (painted green) ● scissors ● glue
yellow card ● paintbrush ● gouache paints ● elastic

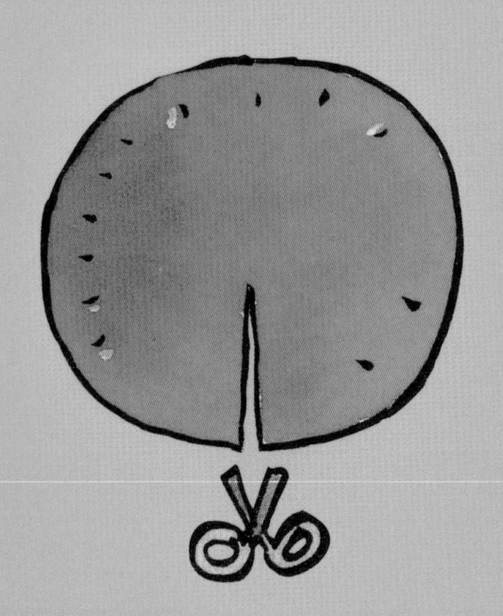

1 Cut a slit in the plate, as shown.

Overlap the two edges by 1 cm. Glue them together.

2 Cut out two circles of yellow card, about 7 cm across. Glue them on to the back of the plate to make eyes.

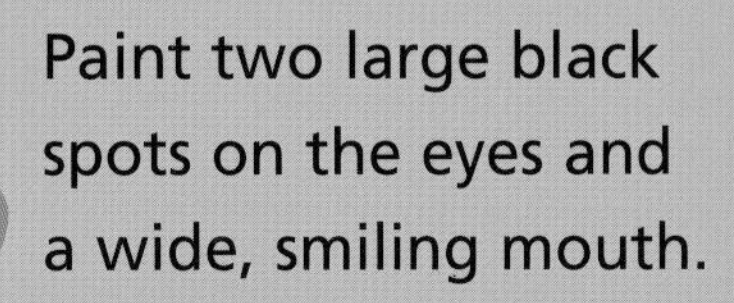

3 Paint two large black spots on the eyes and a wide, smiling mouth.

Put the mask up to your face and ask an adult to mark the position of your eyes. Cut out two small eye holes.

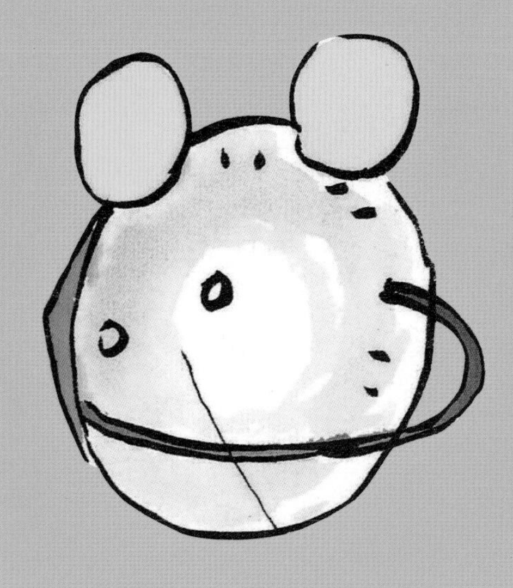

4 Knot the ends of a length of elastic on either side of the mask, just above the eye holes.

Terrifying tiger

tracing paper • pencil • white paper plate • scissors
white card • gouache paints • paintbrush • elastic

1 Trace the nose pattern with tracing paper and draw over the lines on to a paper plate. Draw two eye holes above the nose, 6 cm apart. Cut out the eye holes and nose.

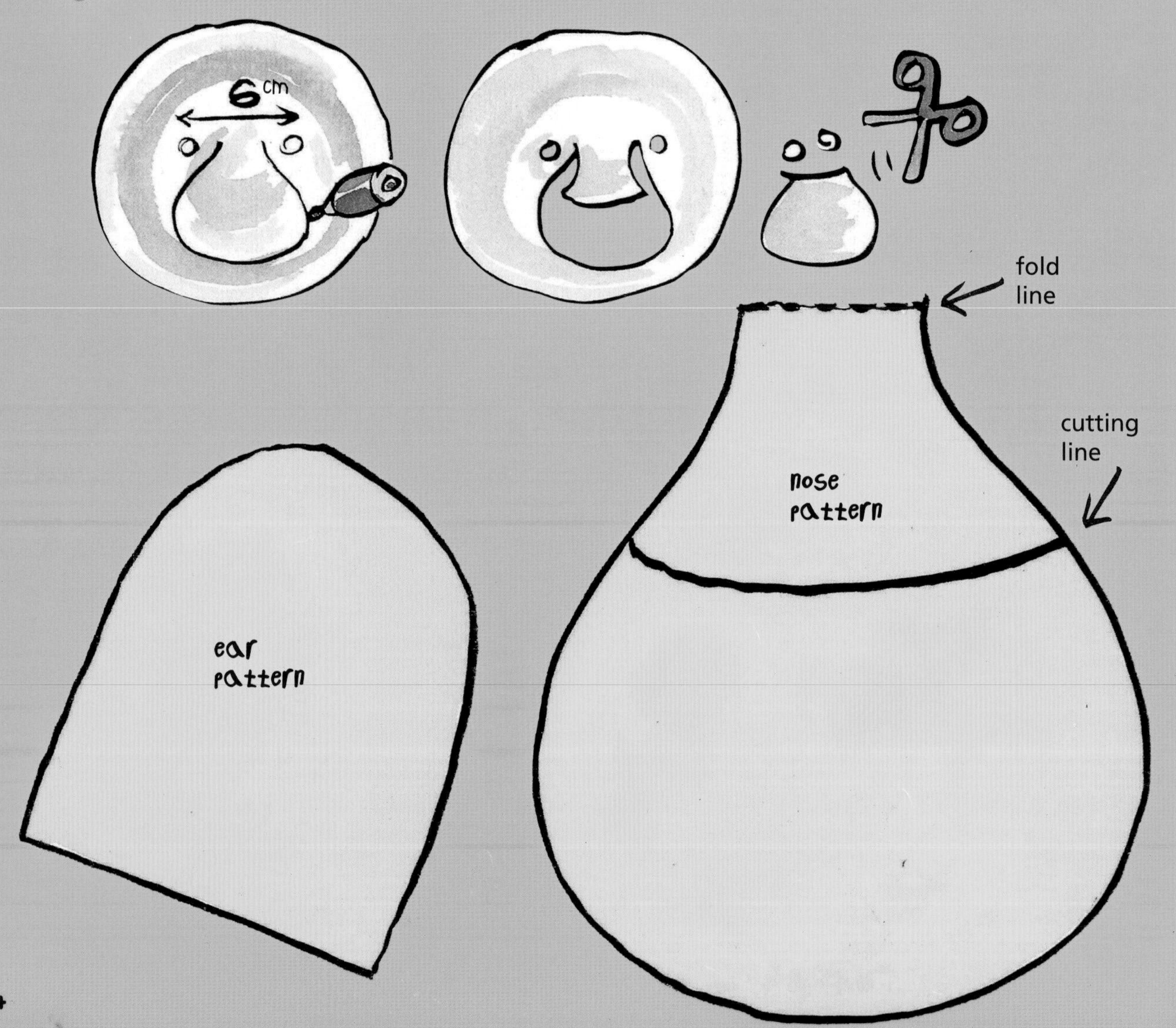

2

Trace the ear pattern. Fold some card in two. Draw over the lines on to the card. Cut out two ears. Glue them on to the back of the plate.

3

Paint the mask yellow all over. Add black stripes and big blue eyes.

4

Knot the ends of a length of elastic on either side of the mask, just above the eye holes.

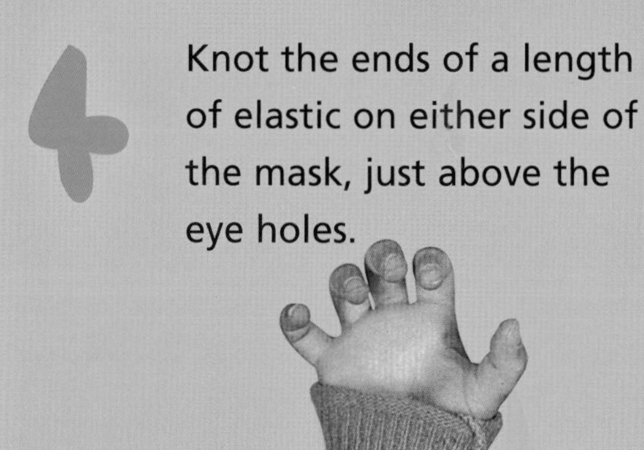

Button King

paper plate • pencil • pin • scissors • glue • ruler
paintbrush • gouache paints • different-sized buttons
painted, corrugated card • wool • jam jar lid

1 Draw a circle in the centre of the paper plate (using a jam jar lid to draw around). Cut out the circle, leaving 2 cm uncut at the top.

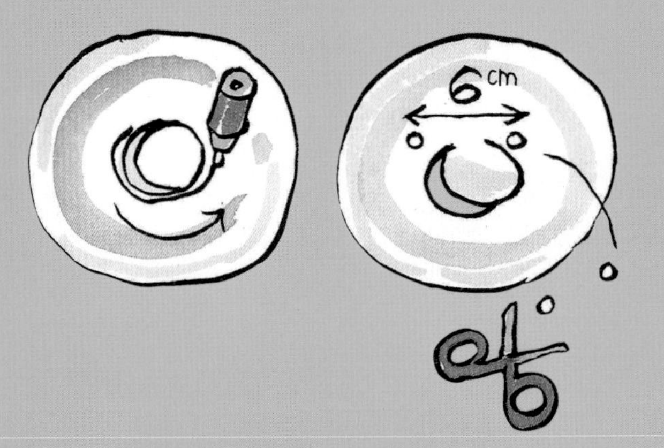

Carefully push out the circle for the nose flap. Make the eyeholes 6 cm apart.

2 Paint the face. Add eyes, a mouth and rosy cheeks.

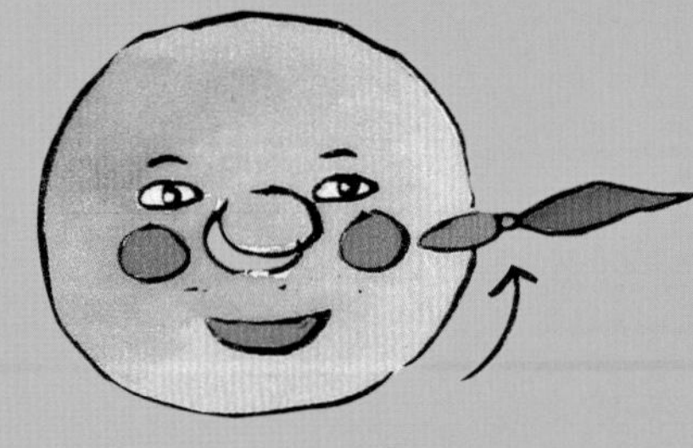

3 Cut a strip of corrugated card, 56 x 10 cm.
Cut v-shapes along one edge. Glue on buttons. Cut short strands of wool. Glue them to the inside of the crown, across the middle 20 cm.

4

Glue the crown (with the hair) on to the mask. Cut long strands of wool for a moustache and glue them on as well.

Fit the crown around your head and ask an adult to glue the ends together.

Colourful Clown

white paper plate • small, red yogurt pot • scissors
glue • gouache paints • paintbrush • coloured card
paper streamer • three polystyrene balls • elastic

1

Cut off the square rim of a red yogurt pot. Place the pot in the centre of a paper plate and draw around it.

Draw a rectangular flap from the top of the circle. Cut out the circle, but leave the flap still attached.

2

Put the plate up to your face and ask an adult to mark the position of your eyes. Cut out two eye holes.

Glue the flap to the inside of the yogurt pot to make a shiny red nose for the funny clown.

3 Paint a clown face on the plate, exaggerating the size of the eyes and the mouth.

4 Cut out a coloured card triangle for the hat. Unroll a streamer. Flatten the loops and glue them on to the hat. Glue on the polystyrene balls. Glue the hat to the top of the plate. Tie some elastic to the mask near the eye holes.

Forest Chief

brown corrugated card • pencil • ruler • scissors
stapler • black felt-tip pen • scissors • toothpicks
a few leaves with stalks • double-sided sticky tape

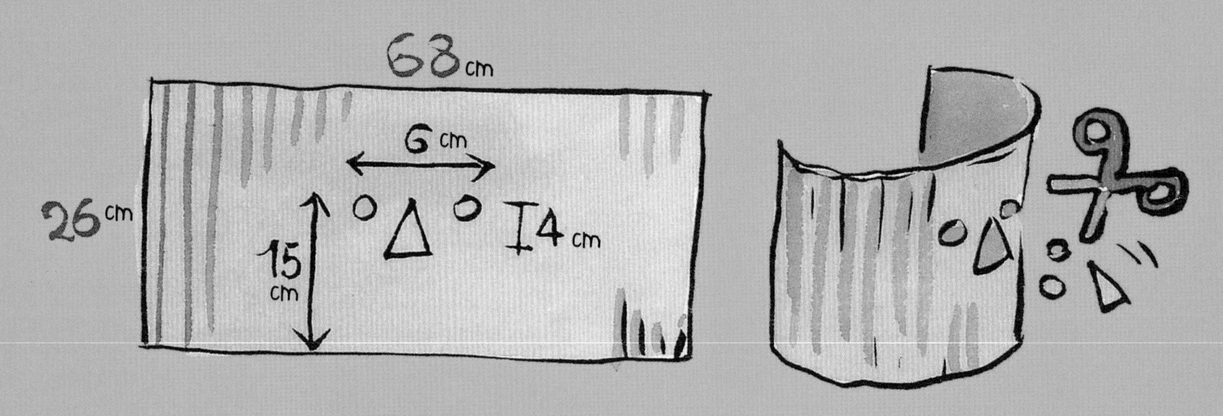

1 Cut a rectangle of corrugated card, sized 68 x 26 cm. Mark eye holes and a nose in the centre of the rectangle, following the measurements above, and cut them out.

2 Bend the card into a cylinder. Staple the ends together at both the top and the bottom.

3 Push the leaf stalks into the top edge of the corrugated card. Alternatively, fit one end of a toothpick into a leaf and push the other end into the card.

4 Outline the eyes with a felt-tip pen. Add leafy eyebrows, cheeks and lips, fixing them in place with double-sided sticky tape.

Pumpkin head

three paper plates • stapler • scissors • paintbrush
gouache paints • black and green card • elastic

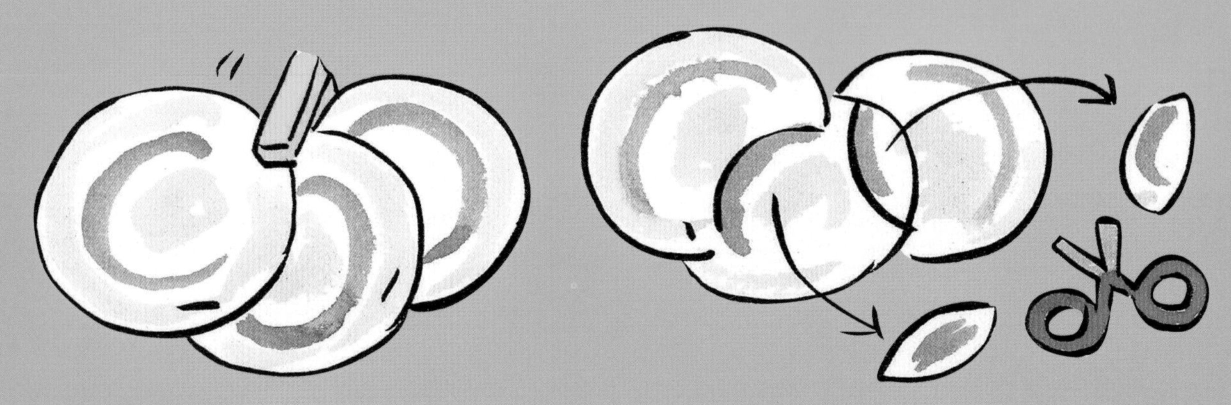

1 Overlap three paper plates and staple them together. To make the mask less bulky, cut off the overlapping bits on the back.

2 Mark the position of the eye holes and cut them out.

3 Paint the plates bright orange. Add a black zigzag for the mouth and two black traingles over the eye holes.

4

Draw a big leaf on green card and a stalk on black card. Cut them out. Glue them on to the mask, above the eyes. Knot some elastic on the back, just below the eye holes.

Sweet fairy

white A4 card ● pencil ● scissors ● gouache paints
paintbrush ● small sweets in shiny wrappers
double-sided sticky tape ● glitter glue ● elastic

1 Draw an eye mask at the bottom of some A4 card, using the eye mask pattern below as a guide. (You will need to flip the pattern to make both eyes). Add a triangle shape above the eyes and cut it all out.

Cut out the eyeholes.

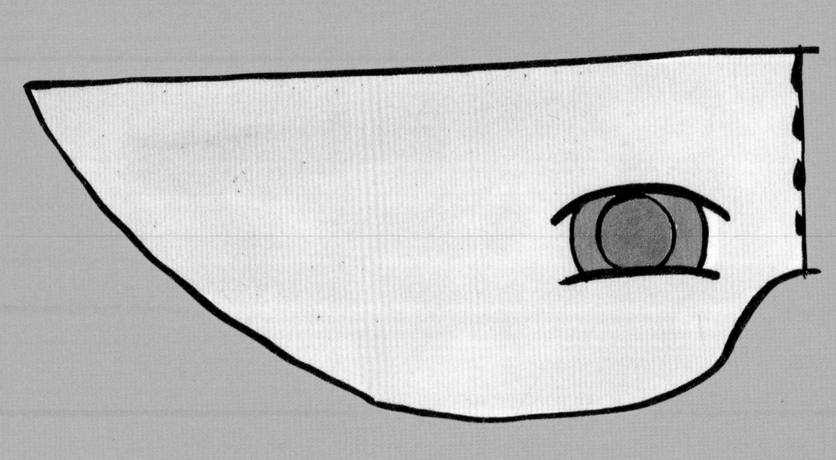

eye mask pattern

2 Paint the face in one colour and the hat in another colour. Paint on large eyes.

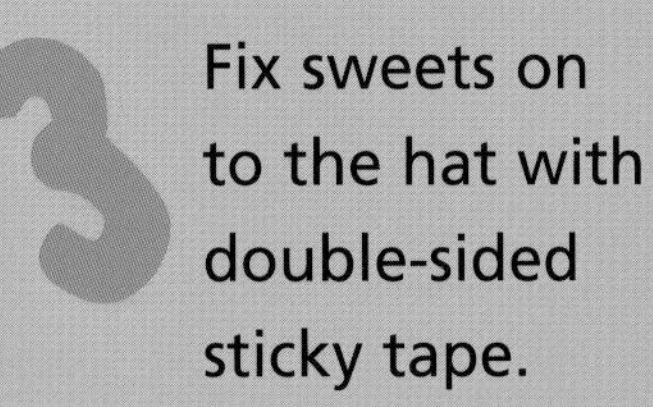

3 Fix sweets on to the hat with double-sided sticky tape.

4 Decorate the hat with spots of glitter glue. Knot the ends of a length of elastic on either side of the mask, just above the eye holes.

Fierce Fly

old colander (if possible with legs) ● two bendy straws
two polystyrene balls ● blue card ● two metal pan scourers
modelling clay or rubber bands ● strong packing tape
thin wire ● glue ● paintbrush ● black paint ● ruler

1 Glue a polystyrene ball on to the bendy end of a straw. Repeat this with another straw. Paint them both black.

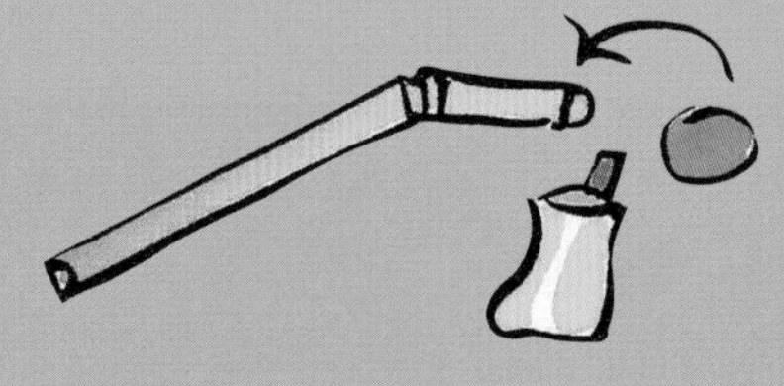

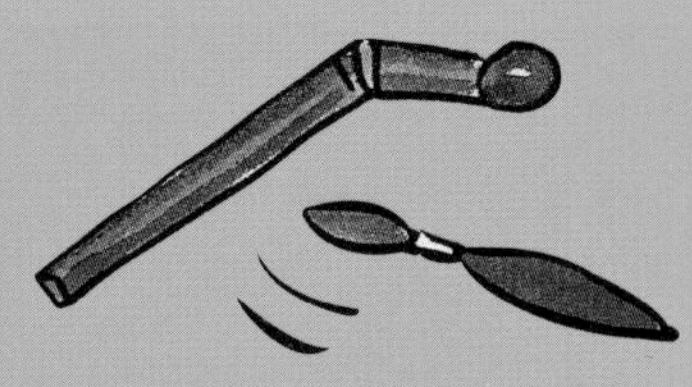

2 Fix the other end of the straws on to the legs of a colander with either modelling clay or rubber bands. If your colander does not have legs you can use wire to attach the straws.

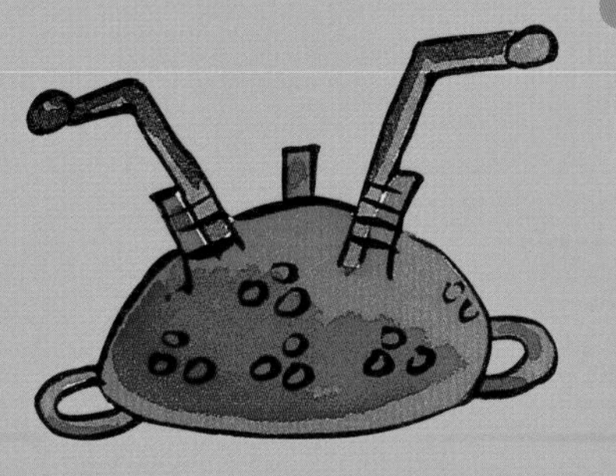

3 Cut four wings (sized 15 cm x 4 cm) from blue card. Fold over their flat end. Fix two wings to each handle of the colander, using modelling clay (or strong packing tape).

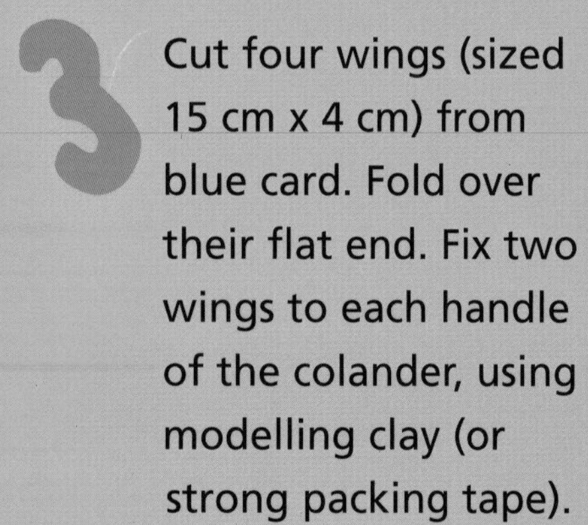

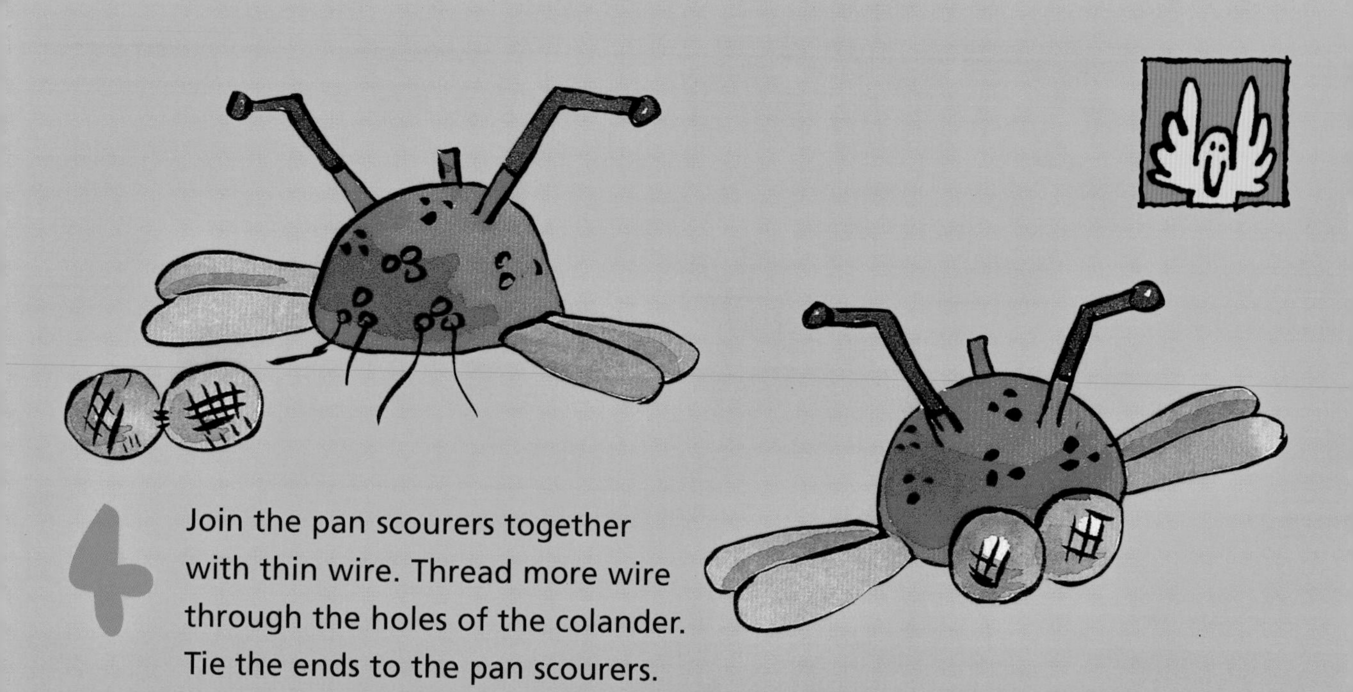

4 Join the pan scourers together with thin wire. Thread more wire through the holes of the colander. Tie the ends to the pan scourers.

Other ideas...

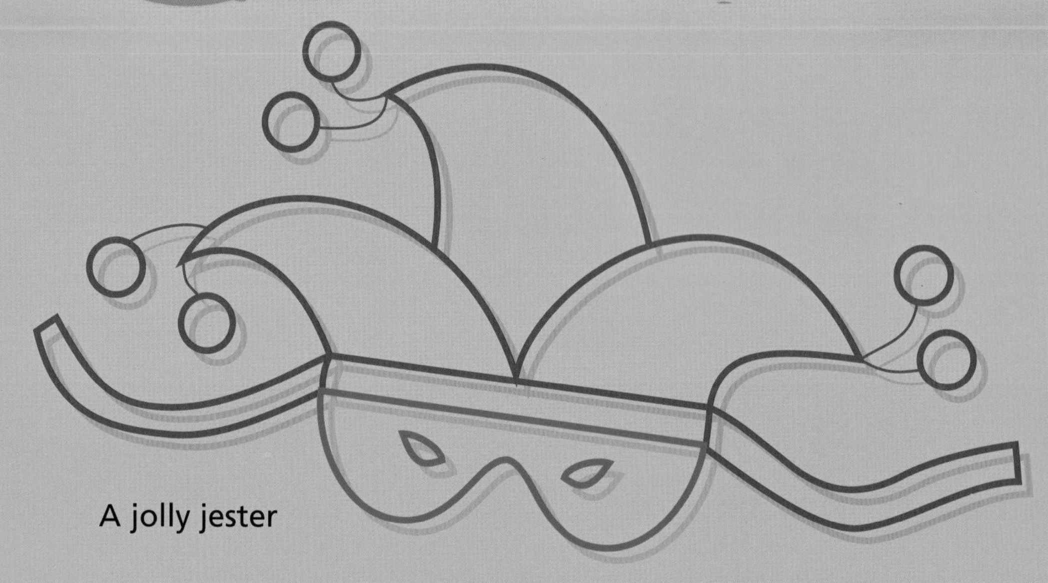

A jolly jester

An Apache chief

Trace this simple eye mask on to some card. Use your imagination to create wild, wacky and wonderful masks of your own.

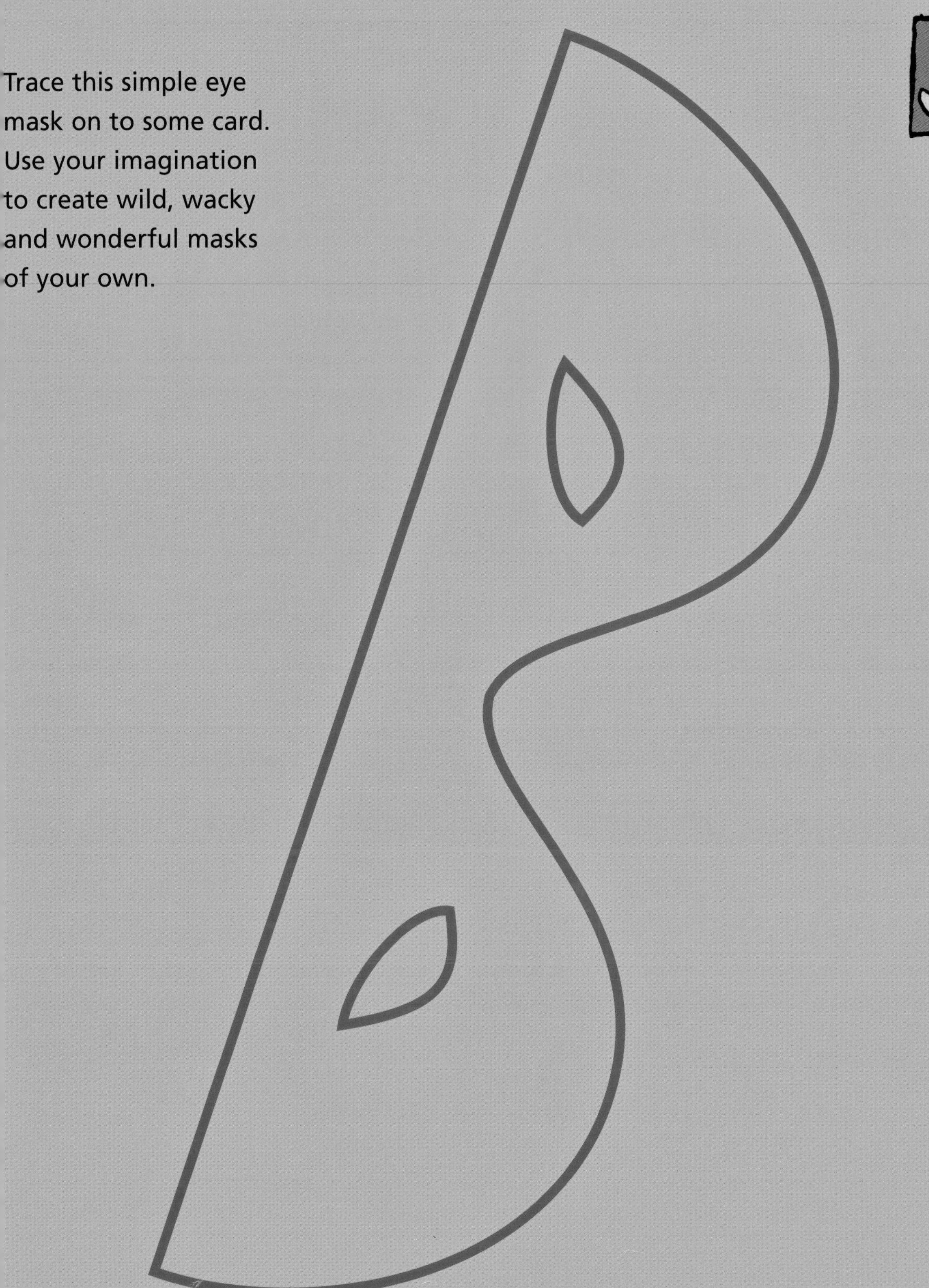

index